Human Nature

Human Nature

poems of witness

by

Albert DeGenova

with a Foreword by Haki R. Madhubuti

© 2024 Albert DeGenova. All rights reserved.
This material may not be reproduced in any form, published,
reprinted, recorded, performed, broadcast,
rewritten or redistributed without
the explicit permission of Albert DeGenova.
All such actions are strictly prohibited by law.

Cover design by Shay Culligan
Cover artwork by Jonathan Franklin
Author photo by Cole DeGenova

ISBN: 978-1-63980-492-4

Kelsay Books
502 South 1040 East, A-119
American Fork, Utah 84003
Kelsaybooks.com

To my sons, Max and Cole

I did my best, it wasn't much
I couldn't feel, so I tried to touch
I've told the truth. I didn't come to fool you.

—Leonard Cohen, "Hallelujah"

Acknowledgments

Thank you to the following publications, in which versions of these poems previously appeared:

After Hours: "Consolation," "Manifesto of the Old Fish" "Once Upon a Best Time"
Bramble: "Things Favorite My Road"
Contemporary Haibun: "Postcard from Berlin"
Crosswinds Press: "Human Nature"
Door County Living: "Wisconsin Gothic"
Door County Pulse: "Human Nature," "Once Upon a Best Time"
East On Central: "Perdition"
Fifth Wednesday Journal: "Among Friends" (Pushcart Prize Nomination)
Flashquake: "Backdoor Postcard" (Haibun Competition First Place Winner, 2011)
Gwendolyn Brooks Open Mic Award Finalist, 2003: "On Memorial Day"
Haibun Today: "Postcard from NYC"
Indigomania: "God Might Be a Potato"
Lifespan Achievement: "Lifetime Achievement Award"
Modern Haibun and Tanka Prose: "Postcard from Prague"
No More Will Fit Into An Evening: "Living History," "Thanksgiving Poem," "We Thought We Could"
Pride: "Brave Pride"
RHINO: "A Day's Work"
Silver Apples: "A Never Confession"
A Slender Thread: "Smile"
Sphericaltabby.com: "Thanksgiving Poem"
Stone Poetry Journal: "Kissing Blackface"

Contents

Foreword by Haki R. Madhubuti	13
Tell the awful truth	19

I

Human Nature	23
Brave Pride	24
Perdition	26
Kissing Blackface	27
Fried Peppers	29
The Privilege Blues	30
Once Upon a Best Time	32
Backdoor Postcard	33
We Thought We Could	34
Nobody Told Me, The Hippy's Lament	36
What Anarchy Sounds Like	37
American Lost Soul	38

II

Lifetime Achievement Award	43
Postcard from NYC	44
Postcard from Las Vegas	45
Postcard from Prague	46
Sunset on the Dome	47
Postcard from Berlin	48
Postcard from Key West	49
Los Abuelos de San Juan	50
Manifesto of the Old Fish	51
Wisconsin Gothic	52
A Day's Work	53
Things Favorite My Road	54
Among Friends	55

Thanksgiving Poem	56
Consolation	58
A Never Confession	59
The Daisies	60
Engine Running	61
The Lonely Sonata	62

III

Living History	67
What Dies with Me	69
On Memorial Day	70
Smile	72
Driftwood	74
Rosary	75
God Might Be a Potato	77
Slant Facts	79

Coda

I am a witness. And we are guilty.	83

Foreword: *The Soul Survives*

Human Nature: poems of witness is a remarkable and wonderful telling of a life in and out of poetry and music, as well as political and cultural struggles. Albert DeGenova's genius rides with him as he travels outside of his comfort zone, whether in Chicago, the other cities and states of the nation, Germany, Prague, or points south of our borders. There are few people in the world as dangerous as a well-read and traveled artist, especially poets with mature ideas and a language to express them in.

DeGenova's work is an answer and a question. His many avenues of notations speak loudly to the many possibilities of betrayal and liberation. He is not a daydreamer fixated on false calculations or on the wordplay of fools trying to impress. These impactful poems are rooted in years of activism, struggle, and institution building. He is a man-poet who, unlike too many of his cultural brothers and sisters, has not accepted a superficial whiteness. In fact, he is a "witness" as in the title poem, a masterwork of political today-ism, unafraid of serious inner examination post-George Floyd.

I have literally read thousands of books of poetry in my many lives of writing, teaching, editing, publishing, street struggle, retreats, and movement politics. It is the one art form that is truly democratic and freeing to young and elder minds looking for answers.

DeGenova's acknowledgment of his own young white privilege is on display in "Perdition" where he writes of his "guilt of indifference" reminds me of where young evil starts, with spit balls thrown at a Black classmate's head by DeGenova's high school running buddies all auditioning for early Klan uniforms.

Yet and yet, he grows up and art, music, poetry, and new friends transform a boy into a culturally conscious man who writes in "American Lost Soul":

> *Guards x-ray my shoes at the airport. My shoes!*
> *I watch Oswald's murder.*
> *I watch a plane fly into a building.*
> *I watch wars like re-runs.*
> *I watch my sister go blind.*
> *I watch my son choke on a lollipop.*
> *I watch intelligent people argue about wearing face masks,*
> *every year a new virus.*
> *I watch a man play golf not 24 hours after burying his wife.*
> *I eat hummus slowly searching for bones with my tongue.*
> *I watch the fire go out, the kindling*
> *is ash.*

There is meaning, memory, dark melody, and family tragedy here. The loud storms of "who are we?" are swimming front and center in a poet ready to face murderers clad in Wall Street bankers', real estate lawyers' and professors' suits.

Less than a third into this enlightening collection are the poems "Lifetime Achievement Award," "Postcard from Prague," "Sunset on the Dome," and "Manifesto of the Old Fish":

> *I prefer the factory cafeteria:*
> *tortillas warming in microwaves,*
> *the aroma of homes, the musical vowels*
> pasar la salsa caliente,
> *the assemblers and packers and shippers laughing*
> *at rest, their full meals unpacked and arranged in front of them.*
> *Here I read books with titles like* Night, *or* Dream Songs,
> *or* Poems *by Elizabeth Bishop,*
> *away from my seat at the conference table*
> *where metaphors are flattened by consensus,*
> *where I am a different class of worker—*
> *working stiffs all, we start at 8 A.M. everyday*
> *everyday.*

Each poem reveals DeGenova as a new world truth utterer who has mastered the absolute necessity of revelatory poetry and originality. Any poet who understands and writes lines like, "holy/Trane's soprano/my favorite things sax" has my vote for poet of the new century. His poetry is a deep divide between information and wisdom, 8-hour shifts and executive lies.

As I read, I am looking deeper for the whys of DeGenova's poems, for what drives this artist/poet of many talents? The poet of "no regrets" who "never lied in my poetry" as he apologizes for upholding the first mission of poets, to tell the truth as one sees, hears, and understands the world as our planet burns:

we are the ancient dirt beneath our feet,
are the Nazis, the Popes, the Michigan Militia,
all the hot dog vendors of Bourbon Street,
we are the President, we are the bombs,
the innocent Black men dead in the street,
the homeless garbage eaters,
we are history—
the waiter delivers our fathers' tabs,
and we pay, we pay.

The poet's work is seldom completed. The old school wordsmiths among us still carry small notepads in our shirt pockets with a writing pen. We forever catch new stanzas and ideas from unexpected sources. The coda of this work brings home for me his final tribute to the thoughts and feelings of his friends and bandmates, two who are Black and did not feel safe in *his* neighborhood of Chicago cops and firemen. He and his family were also denied entry into their exclusive white club. With his "shame faced" he admits to himself:

I'm reading the books too late. Asking questions too late. But I bear witness, white people remain the root of the race problem in America. Awareness today, doesn't erase yesterday's silence.

However, reading, studying, and sharing *Human Nature: poems of witness* makes it for me a new addition to the poetry of Robert Bly, Adrienne Rich, Wendell Berry, Muriel Rukeyser, and countless others who question unrightness approaching real evil. I say *yes* to a poet who is able to write "Satchmo-esque trumpet" and "Kafka's Words" into a poem and make it sing. This is a book for this generation of questioners; it supplies answers to those who put their phones down and read.

—Haki R. Madhubuti

Award-winning poet, University Distinguished Professor Emeritus at Chicago State University, an architect of the Black Arts Movement, and founder of Third World Press.

Tell the awful truth

Not everything that is faced can be changed.
But nothing can be changed until it is faced.
　　　　　　　　　　　—James Baldwin

The day after the presidential election of 2016, needing to indulge my sadness in hot sauce and an illicit beer, I take my lunch hour at Buffalo Wild Wings where I sit within eye-shot of 19 TVs where six different football uniforms parade and battle, where golfers miss putts, where commentators critique last Sunday's quarterback and all the sound on all the TVs is turned down, drowned by a constant dance beat, the lyrics unintelligible in the din of laughter and happy birthday echoing echoing echoing as if the seas didn't part, the tectonic plates didn't shift, the world hasn't begun to spin backward, all our rivers flowing in reverse. The voters are back to their soma of sports and carbohydrates in this *Brave New World* that is not a fiction. I write one true sentence, our only last defense—bear witness.

I

Human Nature

Some will follow the faint trail of blood
through the fresh snow searching
for the story, some
will pay a man with a pickup truck
to remove the carcass—
the deer that ran, a single bullet in its belly,
to die under a pine tree in my woods.

Coyotes in the night
mutilate the hindquarters, scrape out
with sharp-clawed paws
warm organs and entrails. Crows peck and pull
fur and skin down to long white ribs—
the pool of red and purple,
the lifeless eyes of the untouched face.

No one blames the coyote or crow
for their hunger; nor the hunter
thinking he missed, who hoped
to share venison with his family.

Some, though, without hunger
would kneel on the dying neck,
draw a handgun
and shoot fifteen more holes into the hide—
blaming the beautiful doe for something,
something like running.

Some would watch this quietly, some
would cry out, and some would walk away
to let nature take its course.

Brave Pride

We sold our house
to a Black family.
In 1965, in Chicago, when the unwritten
rules were clear,
we broke the covenant.
My father on the run
from the bank, he had no more
buy-now-pay-later excuses.

I believed my father's swagger
his explanations for sneering neighbors:
they were just jealous
of his new TV and his
big car, my mother's fur coat.
His bought-into dreams
discolored and deferred.

Another father
scraping a path out of
housing projects just two blocks away
claimed his piece of a used and tarnished dream—
a simple brick bungalow on a 25-foot lot.
This brave Black family chose
to live among Poles Italians Irish—
on one side a Cuban family so arrogant they refused to speak—
on the other side, a clan of eight kids, including a boy
who ate dirt with a tablespoon in the front yard,
their house so close you could join in their breakfast
conversation—
and next to them
new-world fascists who sent their son out to play
dressed in military uniforms.

Green was the only color
my father saw in front of him,
a family with a proud
down payment clenched
in a strong working man's hand.

Broken, we moved
into a two-bedroom basement apartment
heads down on a rainy October afternoon.

Perdition

Living now
in my father's house of diminished truths,
this is my day of atonement.
I laughed too.
Doe-eyed, soft-voiced Craig Gardner
front row of French class
his full 1974 Afro made an easy target.
My best friend was an excellent shot,
launching tiny crumb-sized wads of paper
from two seats behind Craig.

I laughed though never took aim.
My guilt was indifference
did we know better
crème de la crème
white high school boys
in a Jesuit Chicago prep school.
What was so funny anyway?
Giggling behind the teacher's back.
Craig simply went on with his perfect
prononciation française,
his defense was silent acquiesence.

Craig, never forgive me
(as if you would)—
there must be anger.
When is too late for amends?
my apology now—
perdition is remembering
that privilege to standby.
Never forgive me.
I'm not worthy to receive you.
I've stopped laughing.

Kissing Blackface

*Forgive yourself for not knowing what you didn't know
before you learned it.*
                               —Maya Angelou

Lenore, 17-year old beauty
sexy the way Catholic school girls were sexy
in Chicago in 1973, never said *yes*
to any of my many invitations
but she finally agreed to be my date,
a Halloween party in my best friend's basement—
her promise, a Playboy bunny costume.

She arrived a pillow-bellied Aunt Jemima,
deep red lips and blackface.
Her joke was on me, my schoolboy crush
hung on the lip of a beer can. The guys
laughed, she laughed as we danced
under green and blue lights that couldn't
dim her lie, her rouged lips, her fake-drawl taunts,
    Gonna ask me out again white boy?
I kissed her to spite her as we sank
into an old couch. My ire was unashamed.

Her Mammie mask smeared across my cheeks
I kissed Lenore's wide-smiled insult on the lips,
my nescient defiance of her whiteness
I kissed blackface—
and we are unforgiven.

With a focused and wide lens I search
in and out of all those basement corners repentant
yet the present tense remains a grim confessor.
I dance again and again with that painted devil,

the mortal debate
wrong becomes more wrong
and I go face to face and with my pointed anger
lay bare the shame of my own.

                        Cold memory
clenched-jawed in that old Chicago neighborhood
the ugly shadow still hiding just around every corner.

Fried Peppers

"Italians Need Not Apply"
in this country
where the government Census
couldn't decide what color we were,
where New Orleans lynched us historically,
where we became cannon fodder in a second world war.

Soon, out of the hot southern Italian sun
we got whiter
assimilating that color like a new language.
But at home my grandparents used
old country words, *melanzanna,*
or in Chicago Italian slang *titzoon*—
words that sounded just like the *n-word*
because we weren't digging ditches
or pushing bricks in wheelbarrows
anymore.
We were driving trucks and swinging big teamster sticks.
I heard those words describing
neighborhoods where my young grandparents had lived,
those once Italian Chicago ghettos.

But my mother didn't allow those words
not from her children,
not after her own school days with soaked-through
bag lunches of fried pepper and egg sandwiches,
not after *wop, guinea, dago* labels.
Her revulsion of syntax
a small revolution, recognition
not enough, not yet
    so much deeper than skin
we wipe our greasy fingers
    one cleansing revolution at a time.

The Privilege Blues

What right, this white boy
to play blues, as if
with his shiny saxophone he could
know the Black of blues.

In 1982, alone I listened, waited
for my turn to take a place on stage
at the Kingston Mines
Monday Night Blues Jam.

I kept coming back
week after week alone, but
jamming and sitting in
and being invited on gigs.

I earned a nickname
Bossanova, but not
a spot in the backseat
out in the alley on breaks—

not even after Lefty Diz
announced to packed-house
Saturday night applause
now that boy has the blues,

not when I told Big Gary
with his vintage King tenor sax
You've got "the sound," and he said
but you've got the fire,

especially not after 4 A.M. sore-lip gigs
all night on stage a plastic beer cup at my foot
and breaks of Wild Turkey shots
when I walked haltingly home alone

five blocks to my shared-bathroom
rooming house studio, streetlights
and long shadows, almost
dawn.

No cop ever
pulls up to check my blue eyes
my saxophone case in hand
to accuse *Where ya going, boy?*

Once Upon a Best Time

Walking out of Club Aldonna, 44th and Western Avenue, just chugged 50-cent beers from high ball glasses—Aldonna, a Lithuanian grandma, treats us like her own and says *be good boys*—tonight we are lusting for the Gorgonzola Girls of Bridgeport—we head east on 35th Street, Pete drives, Sandy and me in the backseat, she giggles, she says *see ya later baby*—back at Aldonna's, chrome and black choppers line the sidewalk, we play pool with tattooed, long-haired, bearded bikers who call us *ceegar-smokin-kids,* we bet beers and lose with a laugh—it is summer in Chicago, we are almost high school graduates, we sweat, we talk, plan grand tours of Europe—we've been friends since first grade recess—oh, tonight feels like a celebration!—tonight is blue chalk on black denim jacket—tonight is cold beer and the hard crack of the cue ball as it slams into the eight, the dull thud of the pocket and our long roll along unseen tracks.

> west heading interstate
> a handshake
> the door slams shut

Backdoor Postcard

to Jack Kerouac

I read you Jack, Loud but not so clear anymore—you put the American landscape into words, made it your own. But what did you leave for me in this new century? On your quest for "it"—no mind—transcendence—leaving the post-bomb generation madness behind—as Charlie Parker would close his eyes and blow himself into the shelter of his crazy alto saxophone—Jazz man! you blew yourself into the pages of your notebooks and became the asphalt of sad Rt. 66, the gravel voice of all-night diners, the breath of the hungry wind that blows from San Francisco to New York to Tangiers. You blew your words and brains out with a bottle of cheap wine—where is "it" at now, Old Angel Midnight?

I'm drowning in this new century, Jack—electricity and plastic and Wi-Fi nights of virtual conversation—programmed thinking, programmed wars, programmed music, programmed religion. I'm thirsty for a glass of Grandpa's dago red—Miles is in the sky—my bed was so cold this morning, the thermostat lost its memory—cell phone rings and no one is there, I'm out of signal bars. Gotta go, gotta go, gotta go, we're all gonna fuckin' explode!

                      cold rain, sleepless
                         beard grows
                      whisker by whisker

We Thought We Could

I'll hold the umbrella, your arm
in mine, we'll walk through
the looking glass through the ink-filled rain
through what's left of our meaningful dream,
peer back at our scribbled vanity.
We hide under desks and behind
our tailored cloak of connectedness
and precious handmade chapbooks, it's all
too much lettuce.
Our reality sandwiches are rubber playthings,
those old and dry manifestos.
The barren, poison-tipped
bullets of privilege
are forged of synthesized metals—
where is blind Cupid's golden bow?
Gone like so many mythic dreams
ended. The alarm clock
BuzzBuzzBuzzing—
our awakening out of reach.
We've put the pillows over our heads
with easy posts and angered shares,
outstretched fingers that hope
and fail to touch more, more than
this—this wasted, bombed out Camelot.

Transform malaise, our bourgeois curse,
squeeze wine from intoxicating poems
exalting, exhalted—
taste the prophets
of jazz, of rock 'n' roll
of benevolent science
their golden-ruled breaths
and know again

the black and white of sin's responsibility.
The alarmed alarm shakes
the Yes-We-Can dream that was
America,
no poetry to this dark morning
no trust for a rising sun, I've nothing to offer
but my own confusion caught
between the singing Buddha
and the hot smoking barrel of the dark dyanmo
menacing in the machinery of the night.

Nobody Told Me, The Hippy's Lament

after touching John Lennon's piano at the Rock 'n' Roll Hall of Fame, Cleveland, Ohio

The 21st century schizoid man
is at the door holding a loaded M16.
Standing tall on his camo-clad prosthesis
he blows into his rifle muzzle
fingering a familiar saxophone solo
a song we can hum,
but it ain't rock 'n roll anymore.

*strange days indeed,
most peculiar mama*

We've read all the latest books
follow the recipes for being,
for mystic-muffinhood—we believe that
the soul is as easy to find as the G-spot
*insert two fingers palm up, it feels
like a throbbing ruby shining
in the middle of the forehead.*

We avoid the deadly sins now
though greed inhabits our genetic code—
as instinctive as kissing a nipple.

The country road from Woodstock
is fading, blurry double yellow line
leading us to the hazy horizon, our
vanishing point. We scatter poems
like breadcrumbs, hang guitars
from high tension wires—
still nothing's changed.

Our kids don't know the old songs
and we don't listen anymore.

What Anarchy Sounds Like

Get your ass up on the stage now, gotta rage until you die.
—from the lyric "Lovely Generation" by Cole DeGenova

Anarchy sounds like anger rhymed
with disappointment. Young poets don't write gentle
blue wildflowers, glorious orange sunsets.
They don't have that quiet vocabulary.
This lovely generation wears its words
inked into its skin—black and blue
and red rage; Buddhist symbols
and Gandhi quotes; and leafy ferns
that spread from tailbone, up spine
and over shoulders. It pierces
tender nipples, soft glans—holes
in sensitivity, pain as pleasure,
the irony of this era.
Buried trauma free-versed
on its arms and perfect alabaster legs.

The creed of greed is a lost prayer. Jobless, it
has no dreams to defer. Lied-to, it
trusts its last texts of imagination. Pained, it
splits the differences of parents to sing a new song,
to live in rain forests. We've lost
the flowers in our hair
somewhere along the road of years, we've lost
our children.
Anarchy sounds like the click-click of
Refresh! Refresh! Refresh!

American Lost Soul

1.

Mustang Sally drives a mini-van now
her butterfly tattoo
is a blurred purple moth.

Miles can't swing the blues trapeze
Sonny's crippled saxophone hangs from the ceiling
my toe taps too late, and too often
not at all.

The remains of Jimi's guitars
cleansed of fire and outrage
decorate restaurants from coast to coast.

Louie Prima still sings, *A woman is a woman,
and a man ain't nothin' but a man*
but I just can't make sense of the lyric
anymore.

My old hangouts are pinned to a clothesline—
friends fade
haunted sheets in dying sunlight.

Canvas of test patterns
   can't finish
the picture
anymore.

2.

Guards x-ray my shoes at the airport. My shoes!

I watch Oswald's murder.
I watch a plane fly into a building.
I watch wars like re-runs.
I watch my sister go blind.
I watch my son choke on a lollipop.
I watch intelligent people argue about wearing face masks,
every year a new virus.
I watch a man play golf not 24 hours after burying his wife.
I eat hummus slowly searching for bones with my tongue.
I watch the fire go out, the kindling
is ash.

I stand bare-chested
the rain against my face
black iron fire escape under my shoeless feet
rancorous fists pulling at wet hair
taunting the lightning—

    I dare you
nothing
       touches me
anymore.

II

Lifetime Achievement Award

I want to write a poem that means
nothing, no crack in the universe
no infinite ache, just
a small verse for small
fame, a grain of sand
without an echo, just a breath
fogging a teaspoon, never
to be quoted in a movie or
President's speech, a small
verse that my sons may
remember in late June with
a warm wind blowing
through a café window when
for a small moment
the Côtes du Rhône and the
chocolate crepe taste
as large as life itself.

Postcard from NYC

One hundred degrees today, Manhattan is a clay oven—through the restaurant window I watch women rushing passed in summer attire, bare shoulders and legs glistening, the warm breeze lingering under their skirts—inside, a cheap steak and dry Malbec, an expensive cigar and a leather couch, Jack Daniels neat, wood paneling, jazz trio in a corner next to the bar—piano man oblivious to all except the long-legged waitress, the Black angel smiling, the cool air-conditioned midnight.

>   dark doorway
> greasy brown bag
>   eating alone

Postcard from Las Vegas

A man with a blue face spits chewed Twinkie on his audience—American surrealism, everything HD 3-D, fountains dance in the desert—the Bellagio Hotel's one hundred steel penises shoot water 50 feet into the air in time to "All that Jazz"—pot-bellied businessmen can't dance, their young girls shake tight little booties like it's 1979, while the band hides its musical prowess, smirking behind "Lady Marmalade"—the skirts are shorter than I can ever remember and the legs are so much longer—you're allowed to smoke cigars in bars here—nothing has changed, my fear and loathing is palpable, this *dolce vita*.

Postcard from Prague

Old Town Square built centuries before "jez" music made its way out of Storyville sex houses—feel the sultry steamy sentiments that surround New Orleans in my mind as a band of street musicians play Dixieland with a gravelly Bohemian accent in the center of the square, cobblestones under feet, dumplings in bellies—they overpower the Baroque melodies of a lonely boy with his recorder who plays on a corner near a café where Mozart finds his way through speakers defiantly filling the spaces between breaths of the Satchmo-esque trumpet—and all of this gets the old square's statues of saints, and kings, and musicians, and artists, and heroes closing their eyes, covering their ears—tourists gather at the foot of the Clock Tower, everything stops on the hour, each hour, when the clock performs its magical mechanical dance—its centuries-old dance, bells chiming the irony of time—as in the Gothic torture museum at the foot of a sleeping castle, in the shadows of a palace and cathedral that cast their lofty attitude above the city, as in Kafka's words, in the gypsy violins—the soul survives.

>   the crow doesn't caw
>   riding an updraft, alone
>   into the sun

Sunset on the Dome

Cologne, Germany, Iraq war protest
October 26, 2002

In the Dome Plaza skateboarders spin, curse, jump and
laugh over the crumbling crypt of a Roman governor—
museum remnant of a broken empire—

below the plaza, below these red bricks, the Philharmonic
can hear tourists with their cameras and shopping bags
walking on its roof

the cardinal who yearned to boast his church the biggest
tool of redemption smiles from his sarcophagus
for the clicking shutters, yet doesn't hear

the throng outside the chapel doors
Polizei on motorcycles, in green jumpsuits,
stone-faced, protecting their saints

fathers and sons shouting through megaphones
against this war, another war that worries the wind,
that blows in from somewhere beyond the *Rhein*

that builds around the spires—a tempest of dead Romans,
soldiers and prostitutes panting,
fat old priests eating—

bombs will fall again, empires will fall again
and tourists, stepping over the rubble,
will gather broken bricks for souvenirs
again.

Postcard from Berlin

This city steals my stomach, block after block—spiraling stairs, glass-domed Reich Stadt haunted by blonde-haired ghosts, black wings and swastikas, mirrored axis of this spiral dream-vision illuminating the most feared Parliament in Europe—bombed-out church hunched like a crippled vet with a tin cup—Checkpoint Charlie Museum, gray grained photos, people shot by countrymen, a man left to bleed to death wrapped in barbed wire, dark escape tunnels of Bernauer Strasse—I walk up open stairways, down halls of a bombed-out no-façade building where homeless artists have made beds and studios for 40 years, sold sketches on brown paper bags (50 Deutsche Marks), hawked beer and schnapps from a makeshift broken-plank bar.

It was not sex, it was not joy, it was something else, something I cannot say—when the Wall came down, says Jergen, 70-year-old Berliner tour guide, his teeth knocked out in an East Berlin prison—as a young student reported for something said in a café over cold coffee, among friends. I buy a cement chip of the Wall with authentic, they say, hints of graffiti paint . . . to remember Jerg and his thin hippie beard.

        from the kettle's belly
            screaming
           before tea

Postcard from Key West

Woman with Barbie doll hair plays bongos—rhythms without tempo—locks the small drums between her legs like a Latin lover—her blind eye looks away, the other glares a piercing stare—"illusion delusion, allusion to a dream" she chants at vacationers who rush to the end of the pier—they raise plastic cups, Rum Punch and Margaritas to celebrate the daily Sunset Festival—she raises her empty tip jar, toasting her audience—*Cuba is only 90 miles away, you can swim it,* she urges.

        white gull, dark wind
      driftwood against steel pier

Los Abuelos de San Juan

Under the amber lights of Saturday night,
plantains, sugar cane and coffee on the wind,
viejos gather in the plaza by the bay,
and in a tight ring of folding chairs the *antigua* sing

folk songs. With their guitars, stiff-legged men
strum like teenagers—with their cabassas
and maracas the gathering crowd shakes the rhythm,
with bongos and cajones they feel

the time of their ancestors.
One dark woman in pink ruffles scratches music
on her guiro, another in a wheelchair wears
a black derby and adds the jangling of her tambourine.

In unison these smiling women with
faces of Africa and Spain and mountain Indians,
faces framed with dangling earrings
and pearl beads, sing in Caribbean Spanish

no, es no es de aqui
of lost loves and hard lives in lost centuries,
todos junto their matronly hips
sway to the clave. The ringing clink

clink   clink-clink
of two wooden sticks calls the dance,
tells their sandaled feet where
to move, holds the song in its pace—

steady as the waves under this starry night,
the sea's eternal dance
indifferent to this walled colonial city
to the long dark histories of this old stone pier.

Manifesto of the Old Fish

I prefer the factory cafeteria:
tortillas warming in microwaves,
the aroma of homes, the musical vowels
pasar la salsa caliente,
the assemblers and packers and shippers laughing
at rest, their full meals unpacked and arranged in front of them.
Here I read books with titles like *Night,* or *Dream Songs,*
or *Poems* by Elizabeth Bishop,
away from my seat at the conference table
where metaphors are flattened by consensus,
where I am a different class of worker—
working stiffs all, we start at 8 A.M. everyday
everyday.
I prefer the factory cafeteria
today, as yesterday. I am just that old fish
with five hooks stuck in my lower lip, those misplaced
service pins, broken fishing lines hanging like a wisdom beard,
a gray soul patch that proclaims I am some shape of veteran
a little off-balance maybe, hiding guilt under *bromas afiladas*—
cynicism at the coffee machine.
I prefer the factory cafeteria
but spend my day at the executive conference table, re-writing
the employee handbook as if it were a manifesto, as if to define
any meaning at all.

Wisconsin Gothic

an ekphrastic assignment from Door County Living *magazine, based on a photo by Len Villano*

Where weather knocks with a limestone fist
and each season flavors a workingman's
daily bread with a distinctive salt,
a couple chooses to spend their day off
together in a shanty on the ice.

Where winter blue razors a sharp edge
against a white world, even in this season
there's good eatin'
to be had outta their generous lake.
They sit back—one line, one hole through thick ice.

Inside, the shanty is thick with their morning—
a cooling frying pan, cigarettes,
wet socks drying near the old Jotul stove.
Finished with her beer, her pen and journal,
she is done with words for now.

When the lens focuses on this man
and his barefoot woman,
he glares straight into the camera—interrupted!
But this morning he is forgiving,
he has all he desires, there is enough:
the right tackle, fresh bait, whiskey

and daydreaming about last night—
    Pete singin' the blues at the AC Tap,
        and July
down Route 42   that field
      thousands of blooming sunflowers.

A Day's Work

He chews a black Italian cheroot
tight in his determined bite.
A stiff-legged limp doesn't slow
his steady stride down the alley,
across Grand Ave, across
the tracks to a small patch
of park, to the west-facing bench
where he sits (sometimes turned
away from the spray of the fountain)
and sits, a hand on each knee,
back straight, no slouch. I imagine
he listens to the falling water, this seeming
ancient pond, and hears the city
syncopation of hard-clanging crossing gate
bells, the rumble
of speeding commuter trains.
I do not yet know this kind of work.
He stares where there are no frogs
jumping in. How long he labors
inside this silence, so much living
in this sitting. Remembering—
like lighting his cigar in the wind
match after match after match.

Things Favorite My Road

glareblind between
wiper whoosh wipes
polished asphalt wet
long strokes brushes
on snare drum red and green
amber and white splashing
turning hissss
eee.eee
dark night this
kaleidoscope dizzy
eyes spinning moons of
passing headlights
through measures of holy
Trane's soprano
my favorite things sax
twirls girls in white dresses with
blue satin sashes snowflakes
on my eyelashes blurred
street signs I
my lost home way squint
long road rain night this
am where I

Among Friends

I pour the red wine—
to each guest a personal
toast, the eye to eye
Salute, the glass to glass
clink, the dull sound
of full crystal to full crystal
that does not chime. This

night, the wine is
dark, a fine vintage that asks
ever so discreetly, between
the laughs and stories:
who here this night
has ever hated the morning, who
among this group of friends has thought,

*Tonight I step over
the line, in front of the train?* Whose chair
sinks into the carpet having slipped
your mooring; easier to drink
in silence pretending to listen staring
into the eyes of your friend's wife
than to resist the nagging urge
to watch this repartee from the top of the stairs.

Who steps into the bathroom to stare
into his own wine eyes? How many bottles
between dinner and morning? There are those
among us empty already.
Red rings stain the white satin tablecloth
so many distant planets.

Thanksgiving Poem

Young buck drags
his hindquarters—
eyes wild for escape—
across the unlit road.
The car ahead
had swerved, pulled
  off the road
our friends out of their car
shaking, pacing, *Oh Jeez! Oh Jeez!*
In a field, behind
the struggling, the useless
legs. *Call the police.*
An accident.   Flashlight.   A shot.
Heaving steamy breath. Second
shot. To the head.   Silence.
Policeman pulls
the carcass to the gravel shoulder.
Highway crew's morning pick-up.
Again the moonlight, white
frost, empty fields.

Farther up the highway, a country tavern,
our friend's son, bartender
and chef, serves us
whiskey, no
ice, no flourish—
his friends go
for the carcass, the precious meat
cannot be left
to spoil. Out back
the buck is dressed. The tenderloin
removed and fried with onions

and carrots. A white plate is
passed along the bar
for sharing, thinly-sliced dark-colored
venison, one communal fork. The plate
reaches us, we hesitate
a moment. The taste
is wild, it tastes
like running.

Consolation

We are men, we
touch miles from touch,
shed tears in the dark—
    how it is with this kind
of love. I don't tell how
she massaged my shoulders, my back,
how she made love, or
that there are chilled mornings in March
when I can't get out of bed.
I hold my details in clenched fists
like mortal sins.
              We understand this
kind of silence, almost
shoulder to shoulder we drink
bourbon, float secrets
on ice cubes, our heartbreak
miles from heartbreak
and we sit together,
              together.

A Never Confession

These are secrets that will share my dusty grave. For instance, all the kinky masturbation you inspired. How I should have changed my life for you. How we made love four times a day without guilt. How I miss drinking beer with you at Club Aldonna. How you kissed me more and better. How I saw your deceptions. How wrong it was for you to call your husband from a hotel bed. How your unfaithful days and nights were a hot knife that made two hearts in me: one for my sons only, one for 10,000 gray daydreams. I didn't let you know how beautiful you were the night the wind brought you to me. When you needed me to lead and I didn't. How I've never forgiven you. How you have the most wonderful pussy. How I knew we were soul mates the second you were born. How I never wrote a poem about you. How you were only a notch in my selfish leather belt. How I did change my life for you. How I used your friendship like dirty dollar bills. How I was stoned the night that you told your awful secret. How I hated myself for embarrassing your young enthusiasm. How I spied on you through the tiniest keyholes. I always knew you were lying and did nothing. How I will never admit this to all of yous. How you can't know which you is you. I will never be blessed for these sins despite my regrets. How I have no regrets. How I've never lied in my poetry. I'm sorry.

The Daisies

Valentines rest their heads
bent-necked on the edge
of a crystal vase, petals
dropping on the tablecloth
a chaos chorale of unrequited
questions—
She loves me
not, He loves me.
I am intimate
with loneliness, I do her well.
I have been
her kind, you could say
I have a call
my secrets are become
lost wisdom.
She loves me
not, He loves me,
She forgets me not,
say that I'm your only one,
Babylon sisters—
the daises won't tell.

Engine Running

*... if I in my north room / dance naked ... /
waving my shirt round my head ...*
—William Carlos Williams, "Danse Russe"

Embrace that which cannot
be changed:
gray eyes, height,
loneliness whispering
metaphor lyrics, humming
the *Danse Russe*
my dance of the naked nutcracker,
grotesque gnome, who shall say
I am not the happy genius.
I am best so,
solo, sun in my face, walking
alleys, streets, forests.
Don't hold me this way if you
don't mean it, don't
tempt me from my solitude
alone in the garage
smoking my pipe, blowing smoke rings
radio jazzing,
                engine running

The Lonely Sonata

I. *solo, con dolore*

I've seen the best hearts of my generation destroyed
dragging themselves between the solemn guitar strings
through the foggy pall of indigo streets where no door opens
to a stranger; sitting in coffee shops knowing that
nowhere on a map of anywhere does anyone
sit at a small desk thinking of words to write to them.

Step carefully between the strings of the guitar
    longing to be the persona of someone's poem again
Step carefully between the strings of the guitar
    hoping for someone to please answer the phone on Christmas
    morning
Step carefully between the strings of the guitar
    treasuring the touch of the barber.

II. *scherzo*

So much to do, so much to do
—Water the plants
—Dust the books
—Buy cigarettes
—Masturbate
—Set the alarm clock
—Grieve the red head
—Count shadows
—Take two aspirin
—Pair the socks
—Eat toast and cheese and one cookie
—Listen to the low snore through the wall
—Hear the dew fall
—Dream the neighbor's dream

III. *rondo and coda*

Step carefully between the strings of the guitar
    all is surface tension, a glass filled above the brim
Step carefully, ticks and tocks echo from the ceiling
    the metronome winds down and stops.

Tomorrow is the first day of December.
The sun will set at 4:29 P.M.
Another layer of overcoat.

III

Living History

Hemingway's breath still lingers
here on this street, my street,
his street.
Did he ever walk across
my lawn, sit on my porch
on his way to school, the same school
my sons sit in now?
I walk past his boyhood home,
look up to his third-floor bedroom.
The light is on tonight in that center window.
Whose 17-year-old shadow
contemplates the glory of war?
Do those old floorboards still hold
the crescent moons of his fingernails?
If matter and energy can never be destroyed,
then history is a fishbowl—
we share this same water for eternity.
The song Hemingway hears
as he runs to catch a football
is my voice, my son's piano from our open door—
then, if it's all true
I swim in the same salty Mediterranean
where my grandfathers wash their feet.
I touch the skin of the dead then,
when I write my name in the dust
on my brother's Manhattan bookshelves
and the dead know me, know I am
here—now—trying to taste
their history like a ripe plum
like sour mash, like
all the lovers who've kissed my lover's lips.
We are the ancient dirt beneath our feet,

are the Nazis, the Popes, the Michigan Militia,
all the hot dog vendors of Bourbon Street,
we are the President, we are the bombs,
the innocent Black men dead in the street,
the homeless garbage eaters,
we are history—
the waiter delivers our fathers' tabs,
and we pay, we pay.

What Dies with Me

My G.I. Joe had no Barbie
no *hey Joe* Geisha beauty
no Ken to cook his dinner.
My Joe was a Marine
dressed in camouflaged fatigues
with a red raised scar on his hard
plastic cheek.
I picked a Marine
like my Dad, tougher
than the Army Joe in simple green.
My Joe was a real man,
a man's man
fingers molded in trigger position.
Alone in his pup tent
my Joe piled sandbags around
his machine gun, bandaged himself,
stuck his own I.V.
and bayoneted an enemy
who fit Joe's own brown boots.
I picked a Marine
like my Dad, who proved tougher
than me in my surplus field jacket,
hair well over my collar,
pockets filled with pipe and poems.
My G.I. Joe has served for forty years
in a footlocker in an attic
puffing Lucky Strike smoke rings into the dark.
I salute his broken rubber-band tendons,
dry and brittle, unfixable amputee
arms and feet lost
to the corners of his collectible barracks,
an inheritance my sons will never see.

On Memorial Day

I hear the radio reports,
nostalgia about Pearl Harbor,
and imagine my son drowning in burning oil.
Dulce et decorum est
Pro patria mori
'Nam vets have told me of green and more green
they hated the smell of
green
and brown
brown ear necklaces
of running through trenches shooting at
darkness, of
a year of dysentery
dulce et decorum
I missed the draft by months,
the fluke of a birth date.

sweet and proper
so many Johnnies with their guns
faceless shadows
in napalmed jungles,
on street corners in green fatigues
fading frescoes on crumbling walls.
There is no
saving face.

dulce et decorum
I feel the choke of mustard gas
my lungs burning, the airways
swelling shut . . . turning blue, tears
turning red, turning red tears

a young woman touches
as if someone were touching back
traces a name, a sea of letters
engraved in cold black marble, touches
as if someone were touching back.
dulce et decorum
She leaves a pack of Lucky Strikes.
dulce et decorum
There was no luck.
dulce et decorum
I imagine my son drowning in burning oil.
His blood pooling in desert sand.
dulce et decorum
Memorial Day
the requiem is all the same,
the pain
        goes marching on

Smile

*When there are clouds in the sky, you'll get by
if you smile through your fear and sorrow . . .*
—Charlie Chaplin and John Turner, "Smile" (lyrics)

Bring in the clowns! The lion has
swallowed the trainer's head, the lovely
lady in gold lamé has fallen without a net—
what a mess, what a mess.
C'mon Willy, silly clown
come with your broom to broom up
the shrinking spotlight. Make it good
again, Willy, with your
painted face and whimpering eyes,
your flattened hat hanging
at the back of your balding head.
The Ringling crowd loved their sweet mute
unfortunate tramp—he made them smile.

I slept with my Emmett Kelly "Willy" doll
every night,
gave him hair cuts, took off
his brown jacket made him feel at home,
and somehow lost his hat. Tonight,
I see that sad face on my pillow
in the moist circle of my breath, and know
he is my silent dharma bum,
bodhisattva with grease paint
frown that never straightens or
turns up—even when Emmett smiled,
Willy never could.

At five years old, I held Willy in my arms,
the plastic molded face innocent, god-like
with its red nose. Willy knew—
knew there was no cleaning up
after the fall. No re-shaping the clay
after it hardens. No smile
though your heart is aching.

Driftwood

You've landed
          almost whole

your long Pacific journey ended,
tree roots freed now and windblown
like tired dreadlocks.
How far? from Acapulco, a
fishing village in Cuba? or simply
                          a quiet float

across the Puerto Vallarta Bay?
How far before resting here
your thick branch legs planted
strong in this soft shifting sandbar?
Old Man, we know
              how way leads on to way.

Naked in your grained skin,
bark gone, smooth scars of carved initials
a history in hieroglyphs—
your faded Marine tattoos. No one
sees you resting in the sun,
                    dry, hardened—

sharks and lightning storms,
and glory days
behind us—
waves splashing our feet
                      breath by breath
dreaming of lions

Rosary

I've forgotten now.
The little beads, I think,
are Hail Marys.
Received one as a gift
for my First Holy Communion—
black beads and silver chain,
a special case that snapped to keep it
safe. Long lost,
just as the scapular,
earned then as well,
sacred
reminder of something, gone
even though we were never to take it off,
ever.

Vacation in Puerto Rico,
at the bottom of a hotel pool
someone's scapular is flailing.
I dive in,
retrieve the brown string necklace
stand on the pool ladder
hand held high, holding it
for all to see—
a man runs up to me
grabs it from my hand
kisses it,
sighs
says *gracias*.

It was a blessing, I
think, his *gracias*.
I try to remember
the pang, the missed-breath
effect of kissing a crucifix

as the friar in gray tunic does,
saying his rosary
fingering brown wooden beads
sitting, eyes closed,
across from me at the flight gate
our plane home delayed
by rain
      and thunder.

God Might Be a Potato

How many lies to disguise
the true answer
what does it matter.

I never learned to pray—
not from nuns with their big sticks
and belts of beads

(at funerals for in-law aunts my lips move
to the Lord's Prayer like mumbling
'scuze me to push through a line of strangers),

nor from Jesuits with their black blazers
covered in cigarette ash and arrogance,
who drowned me in pages of Camus.

In a primitive cabin built into a bluff,
spiders and mice crisscross
trails of ciphered verses across a rough wood table—

is it prayer without god?
Condemnation?
Accused of telling truth

facing eternal fires
for praying with pagan insects at sunset,
or the cold back of disgust

for *saying I don't really care
that much* to celebrate
the company's up year

with a rare bottle of Opus One—
there is no music at that party.
Fire me or send me to the guillotine.

I don't care, really. God might be a potato.
Eat them baked or raw
what does it matter

as long as we dance like so many Zorbas
hand in hand, when our dreams and stone walls
fall into the indigo sea.

Slant Facts

I pull my soul up
close to the skin
let it get some sun
or cool in the lake breeze
feel nightfall smooth
as a good bourbon.
Too much?
Better in third person?
He pulls his soul up
close to the skin
so it smells like sweat
and splitting logs
and the smoke of a good wood fire,
up close to the skin
where the sun bleaches
the hair on his soul's wrists
white.
It's not my heart
on a wool sleeve—
this is naked skin
but under the flush,
under the beard, under
the wrinkles of time
under tobacco stains, under the spittle
of words
and in the smell of pencil shavings

I write this in first person
so you
know it is me
even when the facts are slant.

Coda

I am a witness. And we are guilty.

He walked up our front stairs, back straight, confident. Pressed our doorbell with intention, with authority. It was 9 A.M. on a Sunday the day after we moved into our first home, February 1987. A Chicago four-square frame bungalow, backyard, garage, basement—our small dream come true. We answered the door together, my wife's robe wrapped around her 9th-month round belly.

Our Precinct Captain was at the door. The Chicago Machine ran smooth and fast like a Democrat's version of a Cadillac delivering the vote, ensuring the slogan "The City That Works." When you saw a rat in your alley, you'd call the Precinct Captain. He'd show up with a length of 2x4 and perform a grizzly show before calling the abatement crew.

How was your move? niceties finished, he left quickly, didn't want to take up too much of our time, left us his card *just in case we needed anything.* And said, We don't want to see a N(word) in the mayor's office, now do we. He took a breath, *now do we.*

We closed the door, shook our heads and said in perfect unison: *Asshole. He's never met us, he doesn't "know" us.* He only saw our white skin. But we were silent, compliant in our naïve 28-year-old respect for elder, political authority. His power. It wasn't anything we hadn't heard before.

Harold Washington won the Democratic primary. Chicago's first Black mayor was going to get a second term despite the white chrome of that slick Machine. I voted for him.

New baby and settled into our very own house we began having band rehearsals in our basement. But not for long. Our friends and band mates let us know: *It's not safe for us, people are peeking out their curtains.* We hadn't given it a thought, never considered our friends. Shouldn't have been as surprised as we were. *You're safer in my neighborhood than we are here,* Antoine told us. Not such a perfect place for band practice.

For ten years, no invitations, ever, for coffee, a beer, a barbeque. We knew we didn't fit in with Chicago cops and firemen who surrounded us, those Northwest Side neighbors who barely said hello to us. We thought it was because we were artistic, bohemian types. We were marked as N(word)-lovers. It took us another 10 years after we left that neighborhood to finally realize it.

Despite our white blinders our Black friends and band mates never chastised us. Antoine and Marcus knew we couldn't understand. And we didn't. How much we've lost to acceptance. Their rage simmering all the while. Raging against our silence, our ignorance. Now I am embarrassed and shame faced.

I'm reading the books too late. Asking questions too late. But I can bear witness, white people remain the root of the race problem in America. Awareness today, doesn't erase yesterday's silence.

About the Author

Albert DeGenova is an award-winning poet, publisher, and teacher. He is the author of four books of poetry and two chapbooks. His most recent chapbook is *Mama's Blues* from Finishing Line Press. His work has appeared in numerous journals and international anthologies.

DeGenova is the founder of After Hours Press and co-editor of *After Hours* magazine, a journal of Chicago writing and art, which launched in June of 2000. In 2022, After Hours Press, in partnership with the Chicago Literary Hall of Fame and Third World Press, published the highly acclaimed poetry anthology *Wherever I'm At: An Anthology of Chicago Poetry*.

DeGenova received his MFA in Writing from Spalding University in Louisville, Kentucky. He splits his time between the metro Chicago area and Sturgeon Bay, Wisconsin. He is also a blues saxophonist and one-time contributing editor to *Down Beat* magazine. DeGenova works now as Executive Director of Write On, Door County, a non-profit writing center in Wisconsin offering classes, conferences, and author residencies.

Personal Note:

I am grateful for the support and encouragement of Haki R. Madhubuti; my *After Hours* co-editor Pat Hertel; my readers and poet-friends Marci Rae Johnson, Nina Corwin and Patricia McMillen; and my dear sons and family.

I am especially indebted, with my undying gratitude and love, to my best friend and wife Eden for always being in my corner.

—Albert DeGenova

www.ingramcontent.com/pod-product-compliance
Lightning Source LLC
Chambersburg PA
CBHW071011160426
43193CB00012B/2014